Of Love and Loneliness

the recorded thoughts of

Alden

Coffee Table Books
an imprint of GreenWine Family Books

Of Love and Loneliness
the recorded thoughts of ALDEN

Library of Congress Control Number: 2009928351

Swanson, Gale Alden 1939 -
ISBN 978-1-935434-39-9

Subject Codes and Description:
1. POE 00000 Poetry – General; 2. POE 005010 Poetry-American- General; 3. LAN 005580 Language Arts and Disciplines – Composition and Creative Writing – Poetry.

Cover Design by Barton Green

Printed in the United States of America

Published by
GreenWine Family Books™
an imprint of GlobalEdAdvancePress
www.globaledadvance.org

To Paulette, the essence of my love.

Table Of Contents

Of Love And Loneliness

the recorded thoughts of

Alden

Foreword

Men write often of love
and perhaps more often of loneliness,
but rarely of the two together.
Love and loneliness are seldom strangers.
This short collection of poems
threads a fractured web
of love and loneliness.

It occurred to me
that I should write of life.
So I wrote of life and death
and sought to know the difference.
And so I wrote
until I could write no more.

Alden, 2009

have you

have you ever dreamed
when your dream was as elusive
as the blue of an opal
and your world stood still
waiting for it to focus
but it never did

have you ever walked
when your steps were never quite sure
and you thought you were going to fall
and you did

have you ever reached out
to take hold of what you desperately desired
and though you tried to grasp it
you never did

have you ever loved

of life

it occurred to me that i should write of life
and so i wrote
but as i wrote
the fragrance faded
and the warmth became stifling
as doubt smote tranquility with strife

life that ought to be can no more be
for death paralyzes
and yet ties us
to decaying mass and the stale rotting breath
of a pompous form of living death

so i wrote of life and death
and sought to know the difference
that i might hence prepare
lest i should be caught up in the throw
of cold death's senseless damning undertow

and so i wrote until i could write no more
and i searched until i could run no further
and i prayed and prayed and yearned
for some ray of sunshine
to break through the door
but i could not and it did not

alone

alone - have you ever been there
ya that's where
a man can tear
his heart on what has never been
and tis then
that he finds kin
to void emptiness and despair

alone - sure you must have been there
you would swear
no one could care
that your soul itself devours
and powers
dismal showers
of fear beyond that you can bear

alone - where love gives way to hate
hell's sure trait
and men await
with fear that never seems to end
their one friend
death's former trend
the omniscient conspiring fate

alone - where nothingness closes upon itself
and congested expanse precludes help
where city gaiety and laughter converge
to mock your soul's funeral dirge
and companionship ghosts the dread present
until you know not for sure tis you

your search to find out who
would seek this fond life to destroy
brings sure employ
of dark spirits that annoy
fondle and toy
with your determined will
til they fill
you with wanton's chill
to kill
life's vibrant thrill
still

alone - twas not even cursed on infinity
its companionship eternity
mocks of the verity that reality
can be known of itself only
for can there be a sound without an ear
or can immortal soul hear
the cry of your searching lonely heart
and command it depart
except they twain do exist
cursed indeed the quest
upon which the soul is led
in cringing dread
that that which lies beyond
this life's bond
is alone indeed
and speeds
to break life's thread
dead

sunshine

Droplets of dew had formed on the blades of grass. One large drop caught my eye as it began its slow descent to the carpeted meadow. As it moved, it was illuminated by a shaft of sunshine, and a most wonderful thing happened. Magic! Inside the droplet I discovered a whole world of existence - - and I was there, yes, there in the world of my Sunshine.

A darling little girl sat playing. Her eyes - - I can't forget her eyes - - they were as big as saucers and sparkled like a thousand-sided diamond accentuated by psychedelic lighting. She was the ultimate expression of joy and excitement as she handed her creation - - her gift - - to mommy. I watched the sparkle die as her eyes became lakes and riverettes of tears pushed their way through the dust on her tanning cheeks and fell to the ground. Her mud pie was only dirt to mommy. I cried.

A child was walking through the meadow - - hand in hand with her father. As they walked they talked. There were many things she couldn't understand - - and many things he couldn't explain - - but the grip of his hand, the way he said Paula, and the way he talked of God gave her a good feeling. She spotted a flower and ran to pick it for him. Her hair - - fanned by the breeze of her own movement glistened like finely woven threads of gold, copper and bronze mingled together by the hand of an unseen artist - - spoke of the gentleness of her soul. It was just a wild ill-smelling flower, but every part of him showed his gratitude - - it was a gift from her. I smiled.

Their arms around each other's waists, they swing carefreely down the path, the splashing stream echoing their glee. He breaks away and carves her initials on the timeless oak. I see the pleasure in her eyes and the excitement that envelops her and I want to be him - - but I can't quite reach her.

He is untrue - - and I see the pain tearing through her like a trembling fever leaving her empty and alone. I feel the pain.

I see her laughing, singing, and building a home - - but her laughter rings with sorrow and her song is of regret. She lives with him and carries his name for he had taken a part of her that she could not retrieve. So she spoke of love and performed what she remembered of it - - but her memory grew hazy and her acts more difficult. Her eyes are dim and retreating as she gropes for some answer. I reach for her again and, to my utter amazement, I touch Paulette.

And when I do the whole world bursts into a rainbow of happiness. Her eyes sparkle with a thousand sunbursts and I am filled with the happiness of a thousand lifetimes of love. We are one - - and the warm softness of her lips enfolds me with peace. We love. We laugh. We are.

The rocker moves back and forth to the slow rhythm of the lullaby she's humming to the grand-child she's holding. Her long white hair swings gently with the motion. He is moving around in the shadows and I wonder if he is me. I strain to hear her conversation. She says, with a wink, I like butterscotch. I sigh.

me? alone

me, alone - it could never be
for where ever
i look she's there
ready to share
her quiet penetrating glee
and to ignite me
with the inner flame
of love's warm inviting claim

me, alone - i can't believe i
was ever there
in the void where
turmoilous care
allows real life to pass one by
even though he tries
desperately to
do whatever he must do

me, alone - how ridiculous
never you fret
that I might get
past my paulette's
strange power that encircles us
in love's warm terrace
though we are apart
in space   we have but one heart

that oneness draws us together
in love's warm hold
and all behold
i am consoled
by her soft omniscient whisper
that lingers after
we are thrust apart
by the course of the star's chart

her whispers even touch the stars
for the chart soon
has us in tune
lest time should ruin
love's sublime expression and bar
us from our star -
ing roles in love's great –
est drama witnessed to date

me, alone - no never again
i cannot know
where one might go
to perhaps throw
the spell of her immortal claim
nor does the thrill wane
she draws me and i
will never flee her soft sigh

together

i love you   her soft words ling -
er lightly clinging
to the atmosphere of my
mental presence like the sigh
of exotic perfume cry –
ing so timidly
to continue to be

together   the word comes to
express what is true
good and right and enduring
and speaks of a strange stirring
within my deepest being
warmed by her presence
despite the cruel distance

omnipresence   can it be
that while apart we
are together and that no
dimension can start to slow
love's warm charismatic flow
which draws us to our
providential hour

history builds its empires
and each one sires
another   always reaching
out with its wise and searching
means in an effort to bring
the eternal man
and eternal woman

together in one time span
one generation
that history's time dimension
with its cruel separation
that prohibits their one –
ness may be broken
and love may finally win

has it finally happened
history filled and
the generation of love
standing triumphant above
the world's lonely motley drove
paulette it is done
we are forever   one

hell is not of willing souls made

hell is not of willing souls made
through destiny their ills pervade
the evil and the good
until existence should
fain loose itself of them
and hell enlarges its brim

hell is not of willing souls made
for what soul that could would not trade
this dread destitute plight
for the dreamed backward flight
to that creative yore
but hell presses its downward bore

hell is not of willing souls made
tis rather experience frayed
by bad misguided aims
that always curtly blames
its place on things sundry
so hell enlarges its boundary

hell is not of willing souls made
but in time the vital youths fade
life and the flexible
set irreversible
in a cold deathly stale
and cold dark hell draws back its veil

hell is not of willing souls made
but some unseen unconscious blade
carves from our present past

a chain ‘twill time outlast
nor can hereafter rent
hell its fury will ever vent

hell is not of willing souls made
but rather is that final grave
faded experience
and dated common sense
that binds hard to the past
while hell is now more firmly cast

hell is not of willing souls made
even heaven falls to the spade
deterioration
marital love’s ration
wanes and lovers shiver
the real runs hot in hells river

hell is not of willing souls made
of beauty time will surely raid
the compassion and warmth
and make chilling the myth
that existence is real
from the deck’s bottom hell will deal

hell is not of willing souls made
the angels in judgment were weighed
and being thrust below
their curses they seek to throw
by sub-cursing mankind
that in dark hell his place he will find

hell is not of willing souls made
man could easily make the grade
of right choice   proper goal
after the wrong takes toll
but then it is too late
for he is possessed of hell's trait

hell is not of willing souls made
only neglectful ones that bade
the future and the past
to remain to the last
yet the same unchanging
tis in them that hell is raging

crumbling downward the building falls
dying slowly the living calls
to that power beyond
to loose it from death's bond
but 'twas not meant that way
for death and hell together play

time and experience will well
of every heaven make a hell
of the lovely angel
an ultimate devil
and of your life my friend
a hell to others in the end

the saddest words

their love was a bastion of bliss
the now of eternity
the ultimate fantasy
theirs was the fabled magic kiss
that creates fidelity
and where to be is to be
now from his inner being pours
the saddest words
i ever heard
it just doesn't matter anymore

his was the hope of youth and truth
history finally free
and freedom a rhapsody
and he knew that the truth of youth
would enable him to see
beyond the walls that bind me
now he writes in despondent chore
the saddest note
he ever wrote
it just doesn't matter anymore

when love is burned out from within
and the youth and the truth fade
that's when the dreams that once bade
to trust in what had never been
were merchandised in raw trade
death finally life outweighed
from his soul reality tore
the saddest words i ever heard
it just doesn't matter anymore
it just doesn't matter anymore

the rose

i saw a rose all faded dry
i thought for sure i'd pass it by
beneath my feet it gently blew
and i crushed it with my shoe

there from its crushed form then arose
such a fragrance so that i chose
to pick it up and hold it close
to my sad heart   my broken rose

thinking

treasure
tonight i sit thinking of you
and the thorny trails we've come through
together and past hope
that the steep slope
would turn upward
away from hurting toward
the purifying presence of
your simple sincere innocent pure love

hope need be no more
for why should a man hope for that which
he possesses

the curse of love

humans are not the only creatures cursed to love
devils love too you know
their curse is compounded for they seek love above
while yet bound here below

why should the designer make one creature to hate
and in that hatred thrive
yet destine that love it alone should make his fate
better dead than alive

love that blessed curse enables the creature to dream
such dreams that exalt soul
then hovering between heaven and earth he seems
to be held by earth's hold

held to be certain and drawn downward again
until exaltation
itself becomes a recurring curse of dread pain
while its wild course is run

if man could but annihilate the curse of love
he might find happiness
it purports to on mystic wings lift him above
to that ultimate bliss

forever taunting this phantom dove lifts then fades
letting the deceived fall
then all that this fleeting deceiving image bade
will sure the soul appall

treasure

treasure i remember her well
she was pretty
and sixteen
her long golden blond hair fell
past her shoulder
how i longed to hold her

she was delicate and sincere
her talk was soft
and how oft
my ears yearned to again hear
the whispered sigh
of love's eternal tie

and her song the angels harkened
when she sang of
our love
rays of hope broke the darkened
shroud of my quest
and brought me peaceful rest

yes i remember her but where
has she now gone
and upon
whom does she place my lost share
of that something
that promised peace to bring

did i destroy her i suppose
i did but why
must she die
by touching he whom she chose
when she was the
rest to which he did flee

was it that what he needed for
life was what she
could only
give as she cautiously tore
it from herself
he blindly helped himself

while she gave herself to him   he
gave himself to
pursuits   who
drained what he had to freely
give and left him
on the sea of life's whim

when he had nothing more to give
he came to her
very sure
of her will to make him live
but alas she
was as empty as he

strange isn't it   he gave until
he could give no
more and so
she gave until she could will
no sure change in
her now hault condition

sometimes i'm away and lonely
and i hear her
in the blur
of a memory i see
her   and i want
her   god how i want her

perhaps it's love

i've lived my life all the way
everyday
though i never knew certain
the curtain
of life's ultimate drama
i did freak out the trauma
of fear that it might be there

i have moved on satisfied
and i've cried
i've screamed in despair why why
must man try
to reach always past himself
though he couldn't help himself
to know real life of itself

i've laughed in frivolity
gaiety
has mocked my crowded vacuum
i've been dumb
i've known a streak of genius
but i cannot tell what this
feeling that you give me is
perhaps it's love

the autumn of paulette

the crisp autumn chill of time
had turned earth's soft lime
covering to a charred brilliance
that chanced
to dance
before my eyes
and caught the sighs
of my labored upward climb

i had struggled upward through
tender springtime's dew
quite sure that i would find her shortly
and we
would flee
over the crest
of life's high test
and scan the infinite view

but i hadn't found her there
and so i searched where
summer's sun made life more abundant
and sent
a hint
that perhaps she
would never be
so why the desperate care

and though i sorely despaired
i sincerely cared
and kept on searching though my eyes blurred
and stirred
fear's word

that dark blindness
would now find us
forever unacquainted

but the sharp breeze of autumn
aroused in me some
mystical power to reach out more
and tore
the door
from my prison
yes the season
of love was now timely come

the dead leaves lay everywhere
and offered to share
their dying state with my lonesome heart
to start
depart -
ure from warm life
to deathy stif -
ling being without love's share

then at long last i saw it
blazing and brilliant
stung by winter's cold breeze but trying
to bring
life's thing
back between them
the leaf the stem
were one but life had long quit

so she clung to what she thought
was life's source and sought

to find her serenity right there
and share
its flare
with the decay -
ing without weigh -
ing its sure ravaging cost

i reached out and touched the leaf
to lighten the grief
and a most wonderful thing happened
to send
the wind
of winter churn -
ing back to turn
the season into love's glee

everywhere the sun was break -
ing through the clouds tak -
ing away lingering cold and chill
and still
the thrill
had just begun
even the sun
is eclipsed in paulette's wake

like the warm softness of a
light tropical wave
her presence washed away yesterday
today
will stay
always for me
and i will be
forever in her new day

in an instant she was there
as tender and fair
as spring and the surging of life in
the stem
and limb
of the sapling
bent on finding
her own true being to share

and share she did   the meadow
warmed beneath the snow
and everything in nature began
to plan
to fan
the flame of her
love and to stir
the shivering with life's flow

she smiled   the world smiled
with her and styled
its reflection after the spark of
her love
above
exaltation's
pure expression
where even the gods smiled

we ran and skipped   through the
meadow of her glee
she laughed and something deep inside me
leapt free

to be
caught away by
her charming sigh
i came willingly to be

i had helped others to be
in my quest to be
she   in those moments when time stood still
did will
the chill
of my search end -
ed and befriend -
ed my soul passionately

that which i had wanted for
her   she now did for
me and we came to know the way of
that love
true love
that life the more
helps us to soar
to that beyond heaven's door

if it was expressed   that we
together should be
then it must certainly come to pass
that class
and brass
cannot withstand
the endless band
that decrees us one and free

so my darling come close to
my bosom and you
and i will be one and time will nev -
er ev -
er ev -
idence our be -
ing for now we
in our love are eternal

watts bar

watts bar
thou sainted pool of shimmering life
what mystic charm do you possess
that gave you power to bless
her soul though bogged in strife
with new claim to life
and uncover
that of her
that is
his

from far
you brought them to your bank to unite
forever their hearts in one love
and set their gaze far above
the discomposing sight
where wrong is claimed right
by the sanction
of law's one
great tool
rule

from her
you took the gloom that had covered her
beauty and her warmth and vibrance
and gave her another chance
to glow so serenely
that he longs to be
drawn to her side
to abide
with her
there

from him
you took the doubt that love could be real
enough to make two people one
so much one that they would shun
any violation
of their shared love's one -
ness together
him and her
they dare
care

and care
they do and love they forever will
for they have tasted your potion
and they want never to run
from the abiding glow
of that inner flow
and their one mind
to now find
their far
star

and they will for how can paulette's love fail

love's terror

for a thousand lifetimes i had searched for love
then in a moment
her shy charming gaze sent
me grasping for a slight hint
that somewhere in her
lay the power to stir
the unknown in me to cure
my pragmatism and draw my soul to love

i reached and i grasped and was consumed
of her love
i held her and in
desperate moments when
she needed me i have been
something more than i
could ever think that i
could be though i truly try
i hold her and hold for the first time pure love

now i fear that my disparate search for love
has left me tainted
with the air of painted
love-making and my sainted
paulette cannot now
completely believe how
her love holds me like a vow
but it does and i cannot deny her love

the deep terror of my soul is in her love
yes   that which she feels
deeply for me now reels
as her past tries hard to steal
her from the grasp of
my now desperate love
and with mem'ries and rules shove
her away from our discovery   sure love

can i live without her   I think not

man

Alas I have discovered man. When the creator had made the gods and the devils, the universe and the earth, a few scraps there were left - - so tossing them together in a bowl he created a seething pot of the most improbable elements. Thus bubbles forth the awesome and the negligible, the beautiful and the repulsive, love and hate, nobility and poverty. Ho. Thou witches brew. Thou evil angel. Thou saintly devil. Thou are inexcusable, but indestructible.

hell's substitute

While looking for life one day, I saw a beautiful woman. But, alas, she was all body. Without soul. When she opened her mouth, she turned into some-thing less than a woman. Ugly and loud. Was she a woman? No. She must have been hell's substitute. Ah, the body earth can create. Is it not her own, and when it has exhausted itself, will it not there return? But the spirit that makes woman soft, sweet and understanding - - from where comes that? And, cursed man, can you tell me why the beyond has clothed these angels with the same flesh as satan's substitutes? - that man can search sometimes a lifetime without discovering his celestial being.

london

stench, filth and whirling grime
fomenting and lapping together
freed somewhat from the slime
that binds man to a common sewer

freed but a bit and not freed at all
for it hovers too close
to alter the inner putrid squall
of its grim hell-bred dose

it rose to the surface
to pollute the healthful creation
fresh air and sunlight cuss
the unnatural forced relation

while nature itself bemoans its sore
the city reaches out
from its seeping creeping deceased core
the pure and whole to rout

hypocrisy   its soul
flashes her bright lights of temptation
to draw men to the troll
in her black allies of relation

the warm withdrawing glances of love
turn cold and cruel and sharp
when one dares to raise his eyes above
to pierce the smothering tarp

gaiety everywhere
and not a place to find happiness
the countenance is fair
but the soul roils beneath the stress

are none immune to this sucking death
are all cursed to be bound
by the gurgling sputt'ring thus saith
of its hypnotic sound

abscessed and polluted
it froths forth its eminent evil
like the charmed and fluted
potion of the ancient witch's still

until its spell is cast binding sure
poor creatures of the earth
and all the individuals that were
oh cursed collected dearth

life

a spark of life   a twitch of animation
an embryo   an organism is made
born of slime   incarnated of soul
a man   cursed to what destiny to fade

fallen angel   an exalted devil
a demonry   by what mean design is it formed
high aspirations   low inclinations
contradiction   experience churns and swarms

but now the binding sticky slime
yields grudgingly to it upward climb
thrusting its caged spirit free
there appears a lovely lily

chaste and white   pure in soul and mind
not a thought of the filth left behind
love is never surer than
experienced by the virgin

the sun's caress sterile and warm
sooths away the pain of being torn
from the yearning gaping womb
and puts on her a mystic swoon

it draws her ever from the past
upward   onward binding   slowly fast

until gone her sheltering shade
his hot massage will now degrade

deathly wounded she fades and dies
organs aflame and hot breathy sighs
a ball of fire all see
the union of sun and lily

the fire fades
and the heat subsides
life makes a trade
the rose now abides

bred of the sun
the author of life
in one swift run
took lily to wife

now its offspring
ready and aglow
must seek to bring
blitz into her blow

veg'table here
energy inside
hot yearning sears
her red glowing pride

no longer love
in forms soft and mild
no cooing dove
now it must be wild

love's sensation
no not relaxing
turbulent run
a means of searching
the quest is on
hot flushed and yearning
turbulent yawn
passionate burning

the inner life
so all consuming
is with the strife
the body ruining

the thorns appear
her purpose is clear
lovers are rent
love more violent

in her mad search
she spends her body
peddle and perch
growing more shoddy

a hummingbird
fondles and ruffles
her form now blurred
by life's hard shuffle

a bold schism
he there discovers
rhythm   orgasm
again   lovers

nature askew
is it here there's life
only a clue
will stay the death dive

life that something within demands
and yet   still the body decays
on the brink of great ocean strands
ready to sail   soul all ablaze

with gaze upon the distant star
and feet upon sea's murky deep
the soul aspires long and far
until it plunges in death's sleep

to tranquil peace   to flaming hell
annihilation   to what end it thrusts
the body stays   wounded to death
a corpse   a witness to eternal dust

tucson

it's a desert city
with the strange blissful loneliness
that only the desert can create
in its calm certainty
the decades come and slowly pass
witnessing to its eternal state

in quiet turbulence
it smothers 'neath the blazing sun
while the desert devils play its streets
its still atmosphere hints
that when the devils are all gone
calm is restored and turmoil retreats

sheltered by the mountains
the majestic catalinas
she stands the desert's envied princess
her charm consoles and fans
the fevered brows of those who pass
through the desert's heat so relentless

hatched by the last frontier
'midst the swirling echoing sand
of a hot florescent desert night
her heart can know no fear
through ravaging time she must stand
regardless how rough her destined plight

when empires crumble
and are ground to desolation
when history books decay obscurely
resisting the rumble
of mans destructive creation
preserved by the sun she lasts surely

the wonderland in alice

i wonder what wonders await
the man who wanders through the wonderland in alice
is it love or lingering hate
hovering haunting loves once vivifying palace
dare i trespass through the hault gate
does she scorn all who pass only to later tell us
she premeditated their fate
or does she longingly await a mystical kiss
awakening her to life's trait
love that blends body and soul in one celestial bliss

dare i pass to her wonderland
perhaps i shall only trip lightly along her path
perhaps i might but touch her hand
and draw quickly back if it burns with the heat of wrath
so i touch her and as the band
plays a slow dance we know an eternal moment hath
come   we glide o'er tropical sand
and for a moment plunge beneath the waves
of bliss' bath

was it only a passing touch
mirage on the path meandering her wonderland
can a mere mirage possess such
coupled passion that for a moment we understand
not the past but the now we clutch
that the past and the future circle in endless band
awaiting the resolution
of a moment encircled by life's passion to be
can such a cosmic intrusion
be the progeny of something we only seem to see

perhaps   but i wonder what waits
me if i wander through the wonderland in alice

lured

moseying through life one day
i came upon a girl at play
life was obviously hers
for seldom serenity stirs
so warmly in body soul
that i am caught up in her hold

but hold me she has   captured
like frolicking butterflies lured
to irresistible light
diverted from his willing flight
in search of his destiny
to be light and happy and free

held by love's own torturous
fear that love's warming rapturous
pleasure should be denied him
he offers this worshipful hymn
of true confession and plea
at the feet of lovely cindy

lovely is not adequate
to sufficiently express what
this pure celestial being
is and what fraternal feeling
she arouses within me
ah i grab the thought of cindy

she's as fresh as morning dew
as soft as velvet and warm through
and through   how do i know that
by observation   as i sat
watching her move her rhythm
confessed to that fire within

ah but she is cool as well
her glance would not a mortal tell
that she still seeks her lover
for while bound she must hover
until at last destiny
shall cut her free to be cindy

and cindy she'll surely be
for such life as hers must be free
so could it be that i am
that she might know she is to be
and today is for us two
that tomorrow may break on through

fraternity

she came into my life
like fresh mountain breeze
cools the heat tormented desert night
in her the celestial makes its flight
to my lone soul and frees
it from existence's strife

she came   child of the night
to lead me to love's truth
that the night is brighter than the day
where we are in passionate loves sway
for us to live and love
yes it is very right

for souls and not bodies
possess the eternal
quality of love that spawns deep life
and such a life is vibrant and rife
with memories fraternal
that waft softly to please

she came to me and we
reached out together for
a new expression of ourselves
together in oneness we have delved
into the secret core
labeled fraternity

lingering love

she walks softly on the chimes
of time
the rhyme
the music of her body
draws me
slowly
to heavens of memory

she talks softly of the times
that find
us blind
to the world that seems to be
but flees
the glee
that is twain made harmony

she stalks the chambers of my
mind's tie
with by -
gone moments that will never
ever
sever
the now from the times that were

and she discovers for me
the free -
dom e -
minently hidden in her
soul where
thoughts were
born to make me reach for her

i reach and it makes me live
to give
to live
to give the more love to her
to stir
a blurred
life into love's encounter

when i hold paulette i know
the flow -
ing glow
that so electrifies me
can be
for me
wild passion endlessly

and so i hold her always
for days
she stays
clinging always to my mind
my blind -
ness finds
light in the way her love binds

her white hot love

tricia draws me to tranquillity
like none i have ever known
i've aspired the serenity
of congenial love shown
not by the enigma of passion
but by yearning devotion

her magnetic devotion allures
that part of me that transcends
the confinement of life's shackled doors
twisting the real 'til it bends
we implode into her white hot love
elegantly as a dove

who has experienced tranquillity
in passionate affection
what place has tender affinity
in red molten emotion
tricia's serene soft white light of love
surely transcends from above

switzer love goddess

a young god spied a maiden warm and serene
frolicking through a meadow and dancing in the sun
his emotions roiled and he hatched a keen
plan to have the virgin for his own pleasure and fun

commanding now that the sun's warm rays increase
he caused the fair creature to relax recline and sleep
caressing her lightly with dreams of release
he procreated sonya out of infinite deep

the virgin that was awoke and discovered
the passion of love now simmering hot within her
she was never quite sure what force uncovered
her private beauty and warmth
she had sought to keep pure

but be that as it was love's act was complete
and sonya the angelic creature was created
with eyes from a beyond world and lips of heat
a body of beauty with complexion undated

she isn't real   she only appears to be
for never in firm flesh has art so richly reposed
nor can eye bear the immaculate beauty
of which this incorporeal being is now composed

man cannot understand why his blood runs hot
when down his path she chances and her eyes
to him turn
sure he would drink the brew of the witch's pot
if it would cause in her one night's love
for him to burn

her mother wisely bore the unwedded shame
rather than on the heated young god
placing the blame
should man discover switz's love goddess her fame
would defame earthly worship and set
his soul aflame

so sonya my love come now quickly to me
and I will from mere mortals guard closely
your secret
come and to our heaven world we will flee
where all is gentle just you and me and love
my pet

the sunset

a serenade of purple
and blue   of bright lavenders
and red   the sunset lingers
like a cascading ripple
and endless band of singers

a rhapsody   of blue and
purple   of bright red and lav -
enders   its surging glows have
forged the mystical band
of nature's recurring wave

encompassing it beckons
to be encompassed of me
alone   that it and i be
one   one as nature reckons
being in eternity

she was born of the sunset
nature's orgastic ending
rebirthing its beginning
through passion's nocturnal net
now endlessly recurring

her face shown of sunset's blush
her warm passion revealing
a love that sent me reeling
in a trembling giddy rush
of enrapturing feeling

ah   love's rhythmic origin
is now one with my being
heaven's master is keying
our   symphony   begin -
ing our love unending

the essence of tricia's being

the essence of her being
envelops me
in a gentle lingering
longing to be

her essence fills my being
with misty
pleasure tenderly soothing
inspiring me

the essence of her being
whispers softly
tender faith for believing
that we may be

common wife of strangers

looking back i wonder how
i was duped by the vow
of a fremden frau

confidante of foreigners
common wife of strangers
her questing life blurs

what was and is and will be
in tangled fantacy
that can never see

that she can never belong
to one but to the throng
as the passing song

cannot claim the note its own
a momentary tone
that is   but is thrown

to the heap of what has been
for what is   is not when
already it's been

mourning

There is something beautiful about mourning. I do not mean the sunrise. I mean rather the dark hours after great grief. You know the black dress, the black stockings, slow deliberate movement -- all in respect of someone who is no longer. If there is a window from that more ultimate state, the captional satisfaction must be to gaze through and watch the mourning process.

If there is a moment when a woman is more beautiful than in those early days of widow hood, it is only exceeded by the first months of pregnancy or her rapturous moments in pursuit of that condition. Mourning in some instances must surely rival even those moments -- specially in the young widow. There when her passions first miss their satisfaction, she lives in a state of constant approachment to her aesthetics and the memories of her most sensuous moments with her lover. Here in the glow of love play she remains, not thirty or forty minutes, but for weeks. Finally, her amorous faculties spent, she begins to fade.

If the window from the beyond world is not now closed, it must surely be that he that gazes finds great satisfaction in perverted anguish. Like a rose cut from its life stem, she must fade and wither, unless she be grafted anew to some other life stem. For you see woman was made a companion, never to live alone. And if alone, she will surely become something less than woman.

Who would be so cruel as to gaze knowingly upon the light frolicking search of his former mate for another? Not even the stoic bachelor Paul from the early church would begrudge the young widow this wild, frantic grasp at life.

Cruelty sometimes is a subtle ingredient of enjoyment. The cruelty of denial before the final satisfaction intensifies the pleasure to sublime peaks. The cruelty of change gives spice and variety to life. But cruelty that does not yield finally to satisfaction is cruel indeed. The host must surely be twisted who withholds the drinks to increase the thirst to make the drinking more pleasurable - - but, alas, forgets to serve them at all. How eccentric and out of balance is the companion who holds her he left behind with this hypnotic gaze from beyond to release her only after the rose has faded and life is too far gone to draw life.

Cursed be that soul that seeks to live on in more than fond memory. Who but God has the right to bind the world of his absence with schemes to live therein? Like a rampaging city, he destroys all that is beautiful and tranquil, and the clang of his mechanism irritates the tender ears of those left behind.

But, a moment please for the blooming, fragrant rose who chucks the machinery and drinks briefly again of the fountain of youth. She dances, she plays, she frolics in the sun of another morning. Happily she pursues the pleasures of youth that the weighty substance of life had pushed from her. A lover, a meadow, a squeal of delight, and hand in hand they walk from the sunrise.

It must be that mourning was meant for woman for the widower enjoys no such revival of life. But knowing the thorns of the rose hesitates and clings more fondly to the memory of the sweet fragrance. So timid and afraid he sits by the meadow - dreaming and sighing. Perchance a widow, vivacious and living, will seek him out. Alas, nature has turned the table on the lover's game. Night has given way to morning and the warm sun soothes away the hurts of yesterday.

twilight of ardent blue

i close my eyes
and the mist of her presence sighs
the mem'ry of
her fleeting love
lingering, hov -
ering above
the now hollow laughter that dies
in the echo of her good-byes

the subtle blue
of her warm smile draw me through
the misty cool
external jewel
to the warm rule
of love's rajul
whisp'ring my being away to
rajul's twilight of ardent blue

elizabeth

the heavens convulsed and the earth quaked
that dreadful hour the gods mistaked
a spirit created an angel
for an earthling soul
and in flesh did hold
it in its womb-cell
until subdued   no more to rebel

a hard thing for the spirit to take
but you know the gods make no mistake
for if by one oversight they did
all folk would them shun
by definition
they are most splendid
to make them less is less than candid

so the womb clothed her and veiled her sight
lest she look inward and mourn her plight
a dreadful mistake   but lovely too
for now in body
dwells heaven beauty
so serene and true
one embrace warms my eager soul through

mortals in her presence long to be
but she from drab mortals seeks to flee
some earthling might by chance discover
the spirit of life
external and rife

with the desire
to find her soul's equal her lover

there is still yet another story
but we're not sure how he came to be
whether from pits of hell was flung
or in heaven also
they thrust him below
while his spirit clung
to mem'ry where his former state hung

however that was maverick he is
searching and yearning for life like his
a kindred soul who can understand
the hot inner storm
and quietly form
a gentle breeze fanned
by the soft touch of her soothing hand

some saintly mortal once discovered
when between life and death he hovered
that the gods in priestly fashion play
uniting some souls
in marriage that holds
though they twain should stray
and for years mark a separate way

he said 'twas from that ceremony
that love springs which withstands the phony
rites with which mere mortals seek to bind
their fellow creatures
in a time that lures

them while they're yet blind
to the truth that their love they must find

the deliriums of death some claim
but the visions of saints are the same
so could it then be that so it was
that we were made one
in the gods light fun
and all that man does
cannot here now change what always was

how else may i ask can one short gaze
from your deep eyes set my heart ablaze
how in a moment could i so cling
to that fleeting sign
you alone are mine
now my heart can sing
of the bond of that unending ring

though we wander we can never part
in contract you can never give your heart
somewhere my love we will meet again
and there you'll be mine
there will be love fine
gentle inviting
the hope to which we twain must now cling

warming love

love is born of spring
when life is warming
and craves another fling
the sap surges fast
to new brows forming
shade for the lover's blast

all is warm and red
inviting caress
of creatures that had fled
their cold separate ways
their sins they confess
and swear to each their days

for sure spring is love
when charmed by its white dove
but what's to be said
of love that will jell
in winter cold and dead

ah it must be love
boiling and fervent
love of soul and that love
never decaying
lest it should hint
weakness   without saying

love   the which is sparked
by schweiz's love goddess
melts the ice cycles arced
about the cold heart
and her warmth does bless
the lover with springs part

seldom does sister
mother and lover
in one body soul stir
all that is divine
in flesh here hovers
beckoning to be mine

can i not have her
perhaps she's not real
cursed all the dreams that were
if this one's not true
from the gods i'd steal
her for love's one night through

so sonya my love
let not life be chilled
by ascending above
hover close to me
that my life may be filled
embracing thoughts of thee

bliss

beneath the canopy
of tucson's starry milky way
i wished upon a star that alas
somehow infinity
and eternity might betray
the celestial and send me bliss

one night in tennessee
when my wish was long forgotten
a star fell from heaven to tell us
that wise eternity
delayed the answer until when
my bliss could be born as love's alice

she is born of the bliss -
ful loneliness that only the
desert could create in her warm soul
hot and turbulent this
love smothers longing to be free
to unite us in love finally whole

my baby loves me

when my baby loves me
the blue jays chat
the whippoorwill's wail
and the old owl tells a tale
of love's wisdom's penetration of time
with the sublime
truth that paulette's mine

when i love my baby
i'm standing at
the now's tomorrow
where time and the timeless flow
into one bright ceaseless moment of bliss
never to miss
again her warm kiss

a wisp of mountain sunshine

paulette
you're a wisp of mountain sunshine
glistening on the dew
of a new spring morning
you are
the tomorrow of happiness
dawning upon my life
and warming my being

your eyes
hold the mystery of the unknown
like the deep mountain pools
winking back their secrets
your touch
is the soft caresses of the sun
warming the high meadow
generating life

are you
or maybe you only seem to be
are you love's expression
or my own fantasy

the night the gods smiled in zurich town

the lover is the lucky one
but lover without love's no fun
the swiss winter's lonely and cold
the heart yearns for spring to unfold
life was dying slowly i feared
when out of the mist she appeared
the night the gods smiled in zurich town

her eyes were from a beyond world
within them fraternity swirled
her lips of heat and words so sweet
enchanted all she chanced to meet
where has art so richly reposed
where in flesh is love so composed
now the winter's fine in zurich town

from where she came i'm not quite sure
she left me in a fuddled blur
her love can make a man go wild
my circuit shorted when she smiled
'twas there my bachelor complex broke
and those forbidden words i spoke
the night the gods smiled in zurich town

life's equal

life has a way of knowing itself
and of hiding itself
from curious eyes of the existing
whose dull being would sting
it with mediocrity's poison

but when life discovers it equal
it is always equal
to the task of merging life with life
and selectively knif -
ing away the drab cold and binding

so it was that we came together
that we may together
come to know the fullness of what is
that neither hers nor his
will stay but ours will always be

life is in living

she often wished she were
but feared she wasn't
the fear has now brought her
desperations hint
that maybe she has been
but passed herself by
and what ultimate sin
is left but to die

life consists in living
and cannot subsist
in mere passive being
all that is insists
that all is dynamic
and not a thing still
naught of life is static
except in death's chill

so rhythm and beauty
consist hand in hand
and who seeks life must flee
the restricting band
of what was and has been
lest she think she is
until she finally sees
what was hers is his

bernkasteler wine

i sat sipping bernkasteler wine
and its warm glow
sent memories flow -
ing from my minds deep mine
of the time
i first sipped
its magic and tasted hanna's lips

that night   intoxicated by
her welcome glance
i grasp the chance
to gaze into her eyes
her soft sighs
told me of
a young and pure enduring love

i wanted then to possess her
but she was pure
and i was sure
that i could not give her
the endur -
ing pure love
of her youthful visionary dove

but the charm of bernkastel's wine
kept alive in
me her thoughts when
circumstances and time
messed my mind
with other
thoughts and things and sought to cover her

she is always with me though i
miss her sorely
i ever see
her face and hear her sigh
that close by
me she will
remain in love sublime and tranquil

heaven

heaven   yes i was there
for seven wonderful days
where sways
her tender body and bares
sublime thoughts of love
and castles above
mosel's river of romance

and now a timely glance
into my raptured mem'ry
will be
sufficient effort to chance
upon the white dove
of her faultless love
and carry me to her arms again

her love is greater than
the turmoil of earthly cares
and shares
in a gentle breeze to fan
the flame of mem'ry
that sets my soul free
to roam the eons of time in search of her

hanneliese

hanneliese   say it soft
and listen to the sound float
gently down the mosel
from bernkastel
to the end of space
and race
through eternity

hers is a timeless beauty
that lingers in my mem'ry
where words have long since fell
her warming spell
reaches out to hold
my cold
yearning   searching heart

while fate has thrust us apart
and sorrow has flung its dart
of dark lonesome despair
seeking to tear
my sure confidence
that hence
we would love again

i have never ceased to fan
my warm thoughts of you and plan
for that wonderful hour
you would flower
once more in my life
and strife
would vanish from me

hanneliese   the moment
in which i first saw you bent
from your window looking
at me looking
at you half amazed
half crazed
by your charming eyes

has never ceased to be my
claim to immortality
you could make the gods dance
with that first glance
there you took from me
my free
dom and gave me love

somewhere way up there above
where hearts are made one in love
you and i are made one
and being done
it was meant for me
and thee
to come to this hour

so you see hanneliese
the famous mona lisa
has charmed some by her glance
but your eyes dance
with invitation
to run
to your waiting arms

surely it can do no harm
to submit to your warm charm
you see i do love you
and that is true
through eternity
for me
with you is serene

the way of her love

the people were everywhere
at the fair
laughing and playing
shouting and swaying
to the rhythm of festivity
that sets free
the forgotten glee
of their yesterday

excited and light hearted
they started
an old emotion
anew like the one
that captured and dominated me
when first we
briskly strolled to see
the town that dark night

the heavens belched its fury
a flurry
of wet discontent
persuadingly sent
us 'neath the umbrella arms in arms
from whence charms
of love still alarm
me with their mem'ry

that night the glow of your love
shown above
the blackness and turned
night to light that burned
with the brilliance of a thousand lights
to the heights
beyond the frail flights
of man's fantasy

there the elements gave way
to the sway
of the charming queen
of all that is seen
and of all that which is not as well
and the bell
chimes began to swell
as she filled the earth

and suddenly joy was there
everywhere
and the whole world sang
and happiness sprang
from every window and each doorway
to now play
and sing a new way
the way of her love

berchtesgaden

berchtesgaden in the sun
beneath the fluffy
clouds carried by puffy
bursts of wind off the mountain
fresh and clean and light
midst nature's towering might
her eternity is run

in her i see you my dear
your love's duration
and its fresh sensation
touches me softly with cheer
and i feel your strength
as your swaying presence blinks
away lonely life's last tear

i love you

i love you
i love you
i've said it a hundred thousand times
when i knew not what i was saying
and now i am paying
for the desecration
of this one
expression

i say it
i sigh it
but i cannot now make it convey
what i feel inside for you darling
and yet i find i cling
to it   now fully true
my paulette
i love you

my darling
my darling
i have searched long to discover life
and i have   but without you it blurs
to something that endures
rather than that which thrives
now and drives
our lives

to be one
always one
that we might give life to each other
when i say i love you don't let the
weakness of the words be
categorized untrue
i love you
i love you

of paulette's undying love

we are a living miracle
formed of our loving Father
from her
undying
love abiding
flowing from her pure longing soul

help us oh Father to know your
divine pleasure in our lives
that strives
to form us
transforming thus
to thy purpose holy and pure

thank you our loving Father
that now in your holy union
we're one
living soul
insep'rable
as our love in you is pure

OF LOVE AND LONELINESS
the recorded thoughts of ALDEN

ISBN 978-1-935434-39-9

Coffee Table Books
an imprint of GreenWine Family Books

www.ingramcontent.com/pod-product-compliance
Lightning Source LLC
LaVergne TN
LVHW011428080426
835512LV00005B/324